TWELVE**FOLK**SONGS FOR**GUITAR**ENSEMBLE

Folk Music of the United Kingdom and Ireland Arranged For Guitar Ensemble

PAUL**KEAN**

FUNDAMENTAL**CHANGES**

Twelve Folk Songs For Guitar Ensemble

Folk Music of the United Kingdom and Ireland Arranged For Guitar Ensemble

Published by www.fundamental-changes.com

ISBN 978-1-78933-077-9

Copyright © 2019 Paul Kean

The moral right of this author has been asserted.

All rights reserved. No part of this publication may be reproduced, stored in a retrieval system, or transmitted in any form or by any means, without the prior permission in writing from the publisher.

The publisher is not responsible for websites (or their content) that are not owned by the publisher.

www.fundamental-changes.com

Twitter: **@guitar_joseph**

Over 10,000 fans on Facebook: **FundamentalChangesInGuitar**

Instagram: **FundamentalChanges**

For over 350 Free Guitar Lessons with Videos Check Out

www.fundamental-changes.com

Image Copyright: Shutterstock 512r

Contents

Foreword	4
Introduction	5

ENGLAND

What Shall We Do With the Drunken Sailor?	6
The Cutty Wren	14
The Miller of Dee	22

IRELAND

Molly Malone	32
The Irish Washerwoman	40
The Last Rose of Summer	48

SCOTLAND

Iona Boat Song	56
Loch Lomond	64
The Blantyre Explosion	72

WALES

All Through the Night	78
Land of My Fathers	82
The Ash Grove	90

Other Books from Fundamental Changes	98

Foreword

Despite the obvious success and popularity of the guitar, there is a surprising shortage of quality ensemble material which is both musically satisfying and educationally well-conceived. Paul Kean is well equipped for the task of producing such material, being an exceptionally gifted and highly experienced teacher, and well-qualified guitarist.

Indigenous British folk songs provide good vehicles for this purpose as they are melodically memorable, harmonically satisfying, and basic in form and overall architecture. This makes them an ideal format for the experienced teacher to introduce various aspects of technique in a thoughtful, incremental manner. Paul Kean has succeeded admirably in doing so.

It is a pity that such folk music – which, after all, provided the background for the early 20th century *Pastoral* movement and went on to become a staple of the BBC music for schools *Singing Together* series – has lost favour in recent years. Full marks to Paul Kean for re-discovering their educational potential.

Adrian Ingram MA, MPhil, FTCL, FLCM, Cert Ed

Introduction

This volume is a companion to my first book, *Ten Classical Pieces for Guitar Ensemble*. The aim of the series is to provide a resource for guitar teachers and groups who wish to develop their ensemble skills, and who want to experience the joy and challenge of group music making.

In this book you will find twelve folk tunes from Britain and Ireland, all arranged in three parts. The pieces are designed to be accessible to most players. Some, like *All Through the Night*, are simple and straightforward. Others, such as *The Miller of Dee*, may require more work to produce a convincing performance.

Students of the guitar often spend much of their time practising alone or jamming with friends. While this is eminently worthwhile, one can pick up bad musical habits and neglect certain basic skills that all musicians need. These shortcomings often become apparent when playing as part of an ensemble. I therefore offer the following tips:

- Know your own part thoroughly.

- Play what the music tells you to play. Other parts may be very different to yours and it is sometimes tempting to follow others.

- Always aim to produce a good tone, even when you are providing background accompaniment.

- Always set the tempo before you begin a piece.

- Ensure that you begin and end your parts cleanly.

- Follow the dynamic instructions

- Know your role at all times. You may have to switch from playing a prominent melody, to a less prominent accompaniment and adjust how you play accordingly.

- If your group is struggling with a particular section of a song, isolate that section and practise it on its own.

- Aim to sound convincing and engaging from the very first note.

- Try to hear all the parts as you play, in order to perform as a tight unit.

And, most importantly:

- If you make a mistake, look askance at the player next to you. Then the audience may think it was them!

Happy playing,

Paul

Part 1 # What Shall We Do With The Drunken Sailor?

English traditional

Allegretto

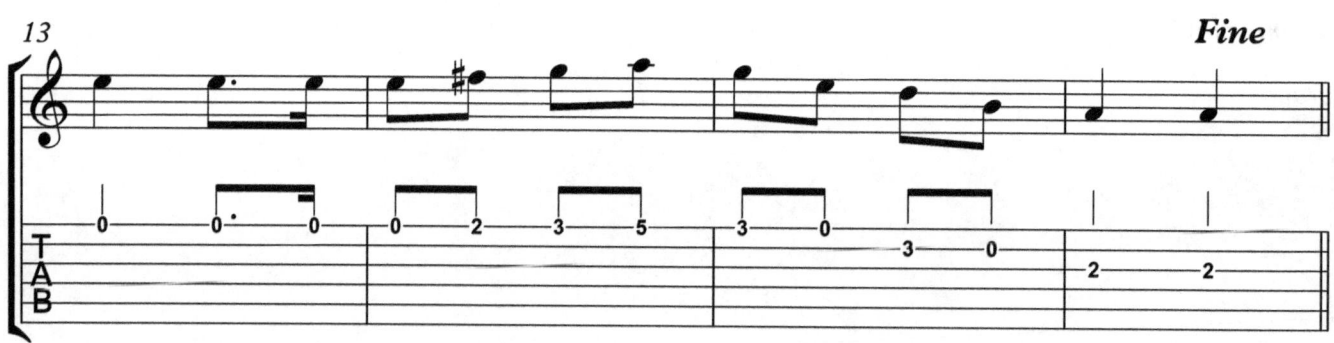

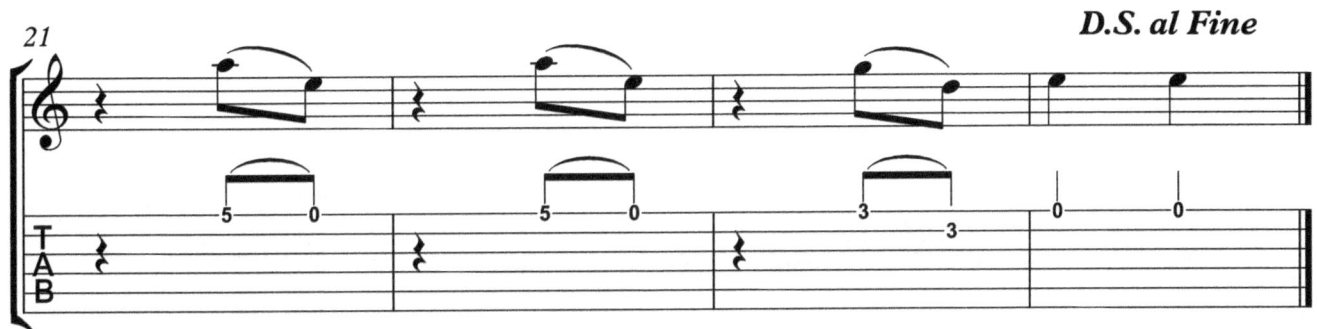

D.S. al Fine

7

Part 2 # What Shall We Do With The Drunken Sailor?

English traditional

Part 3 # What Shall We Do With The Drunken Sailor?

English traditional

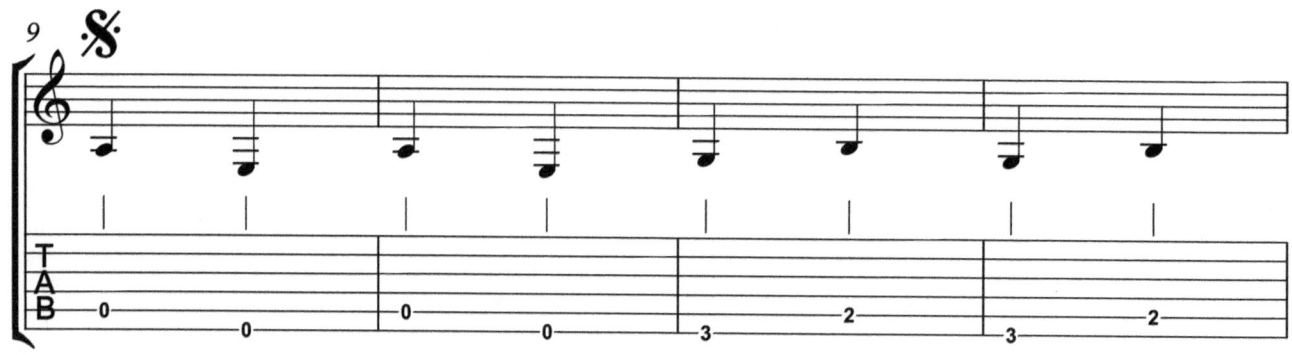

What Shall We Do With The Drunken Sailor?

Score

English traditional

Part 1

The Cutty Wren

English traditional

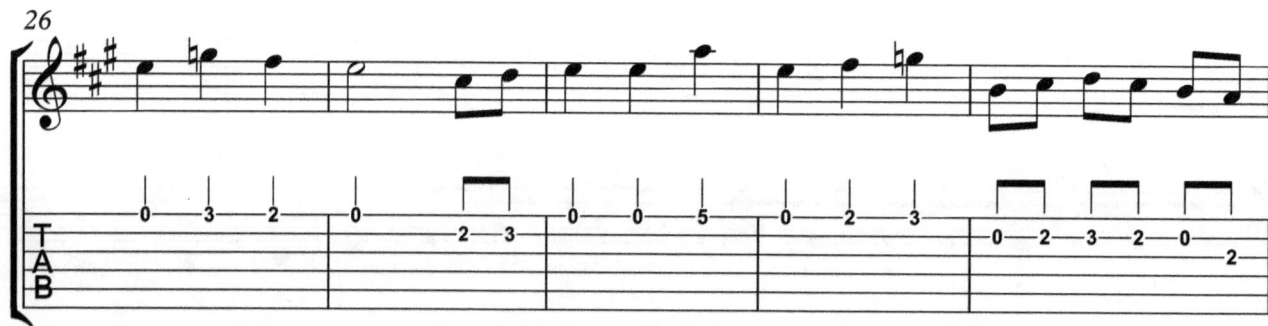

2

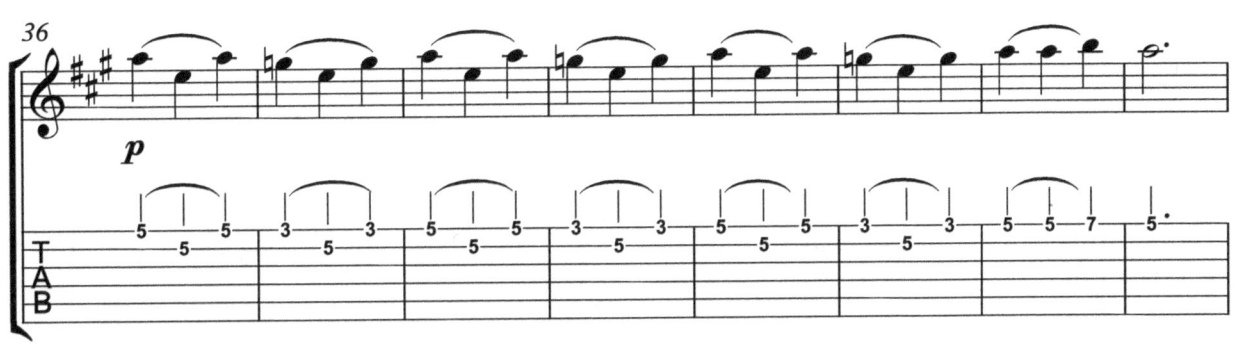

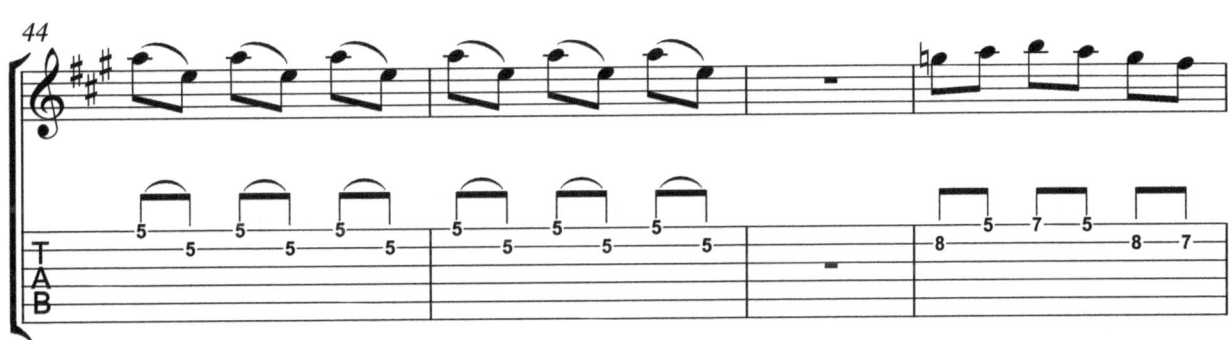

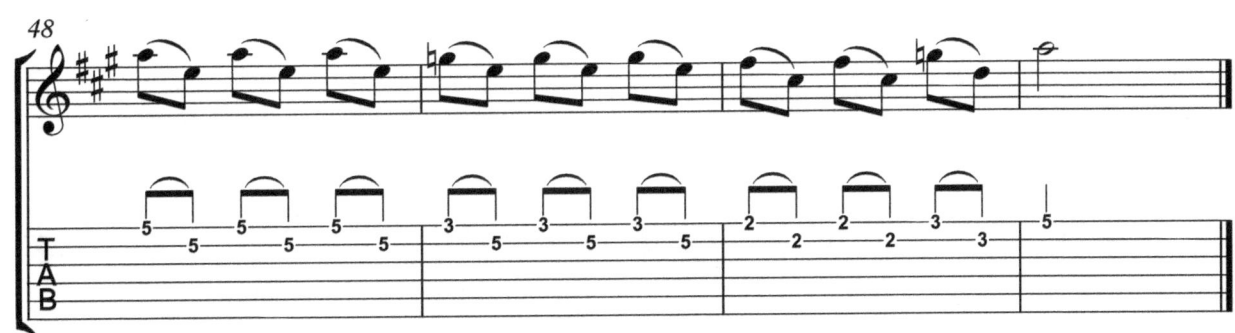

15

Part 2

The Cutty Wren

English traditional

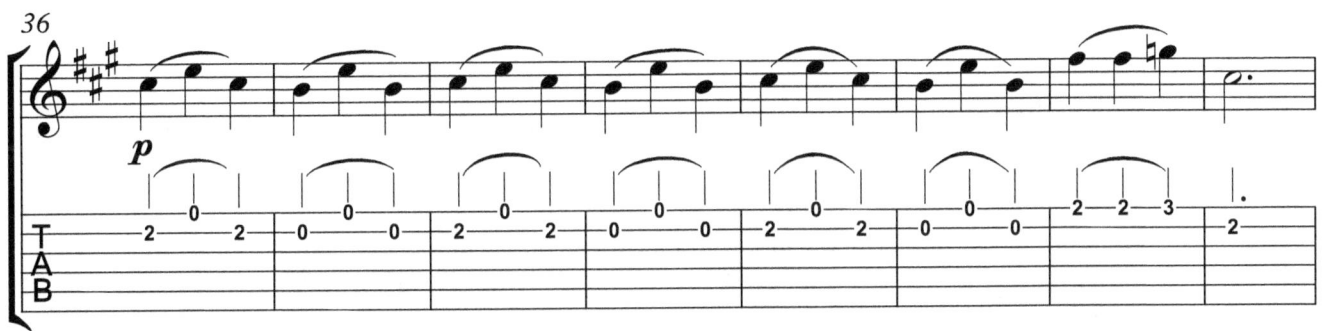

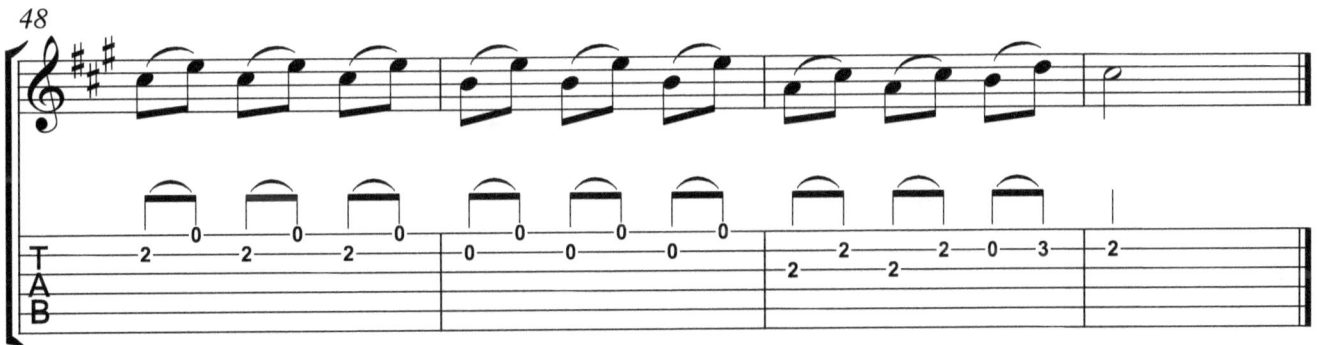

Part 3

The Cutty Wren

English traditional

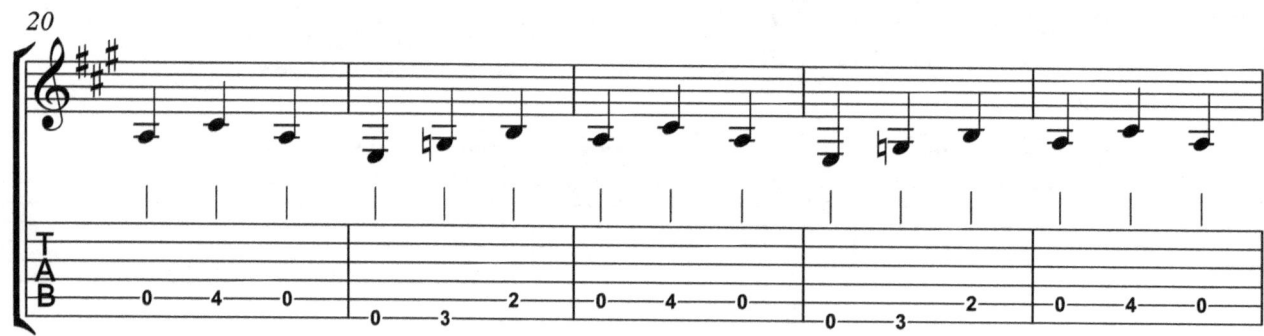

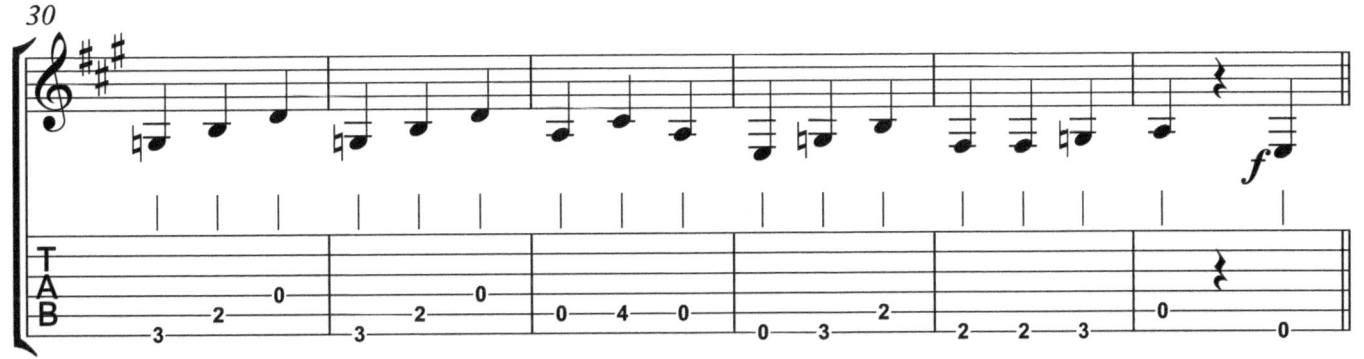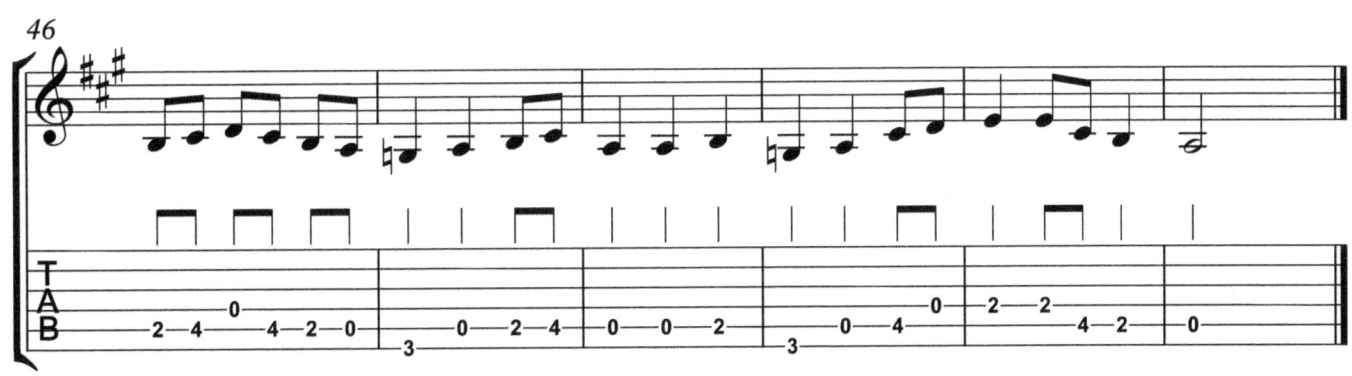

The Cutty Wren

English traditional

Part 1

The Miller of Dee

English traditional

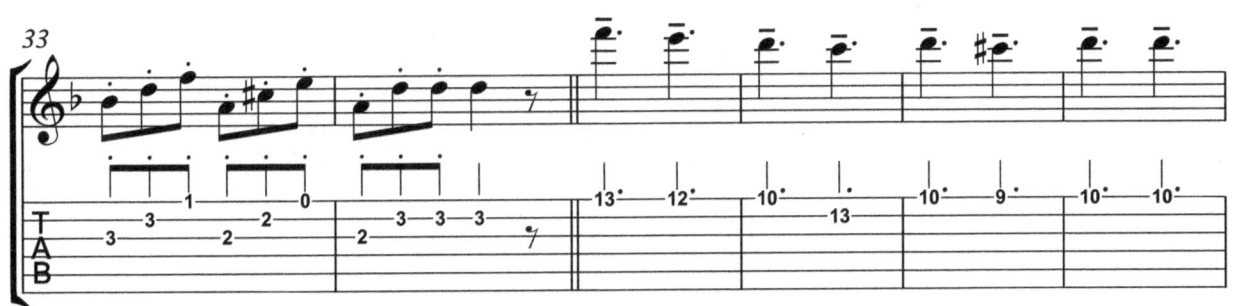
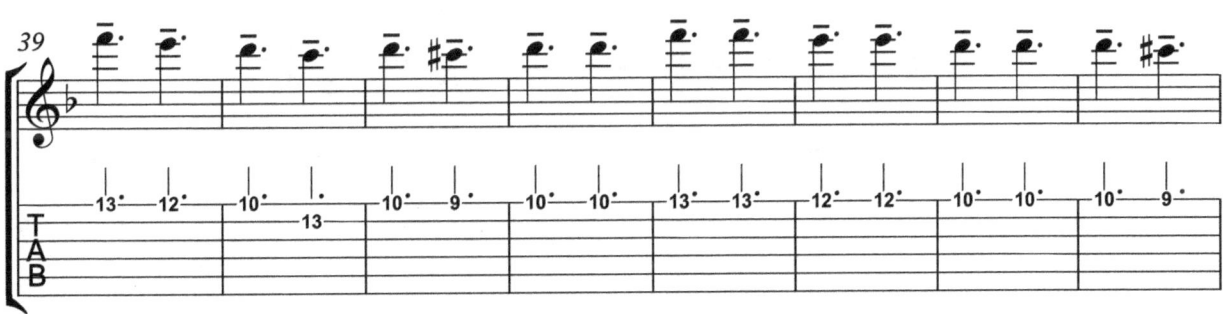

D.C. al Coda

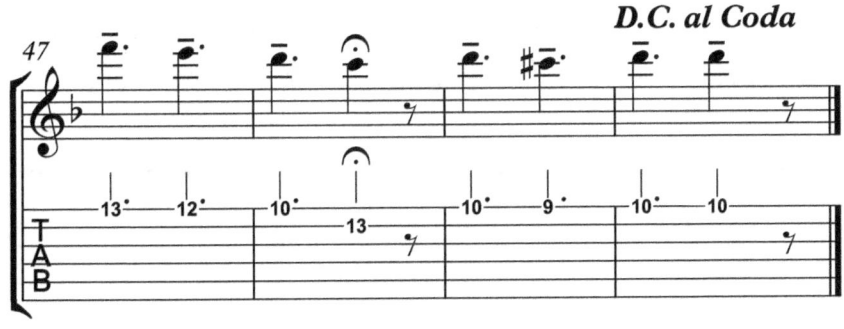

Part 2

The Miller of Dee

English traditional

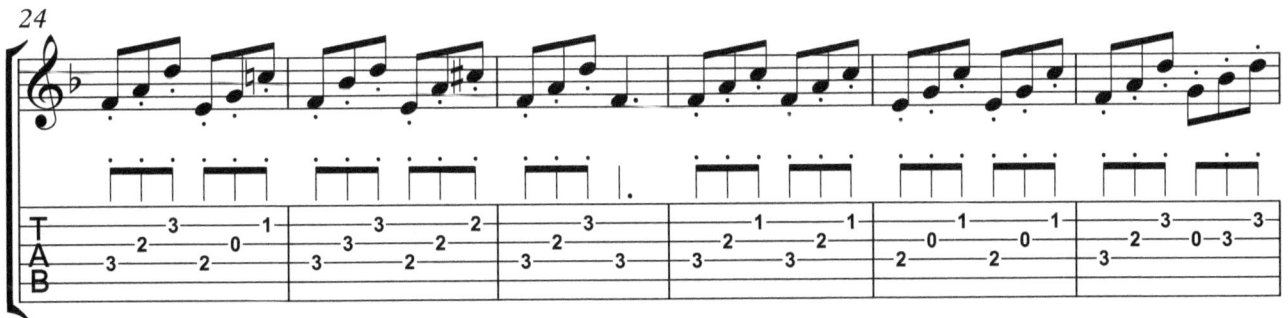

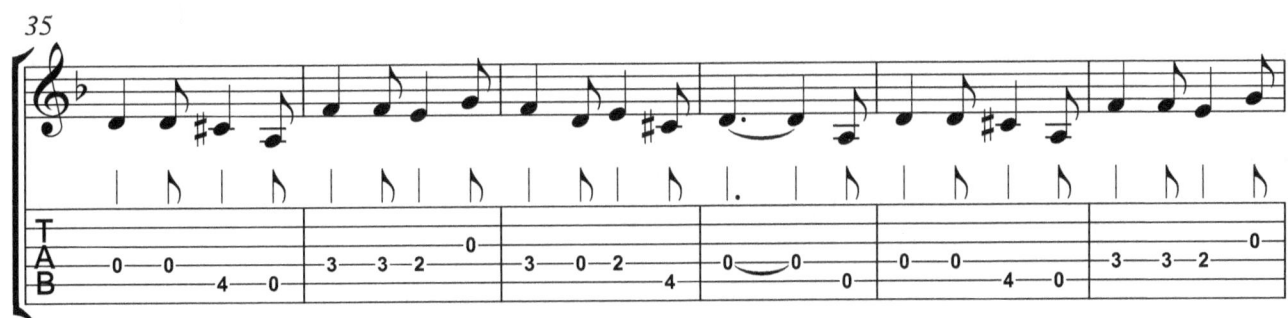

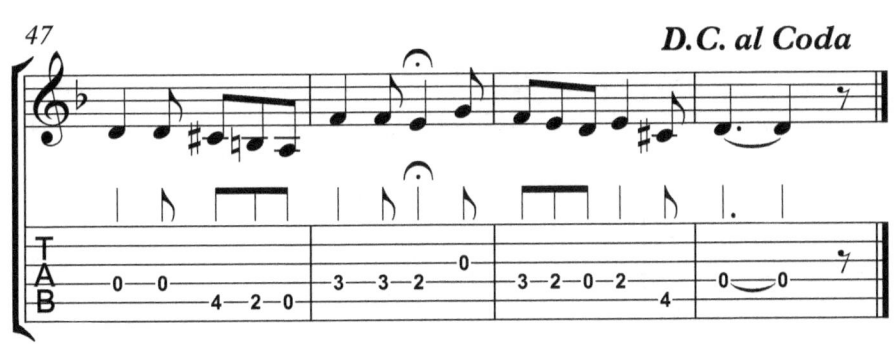

D.C. al Coda

Part 3

The Miller of Dee

English traditional

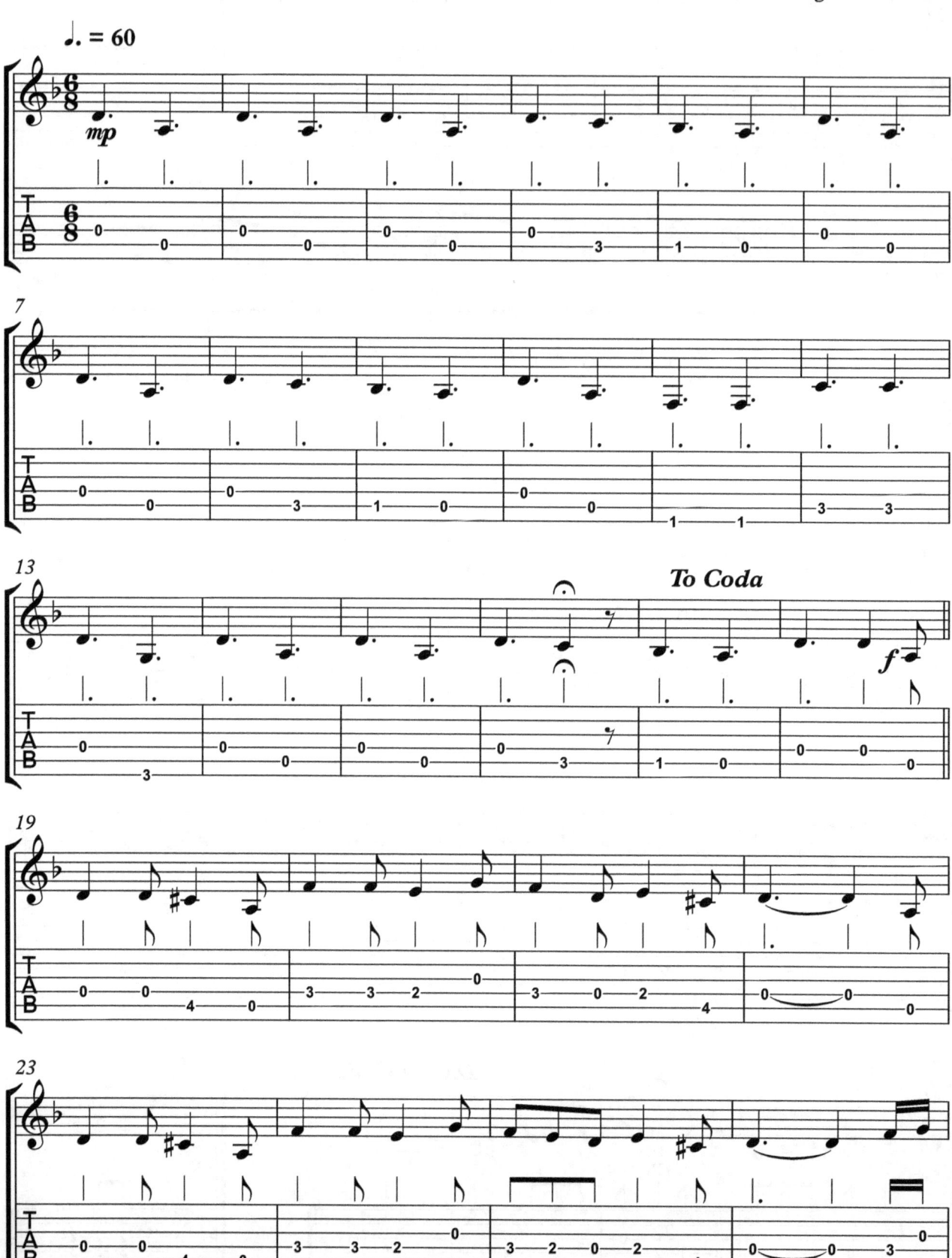

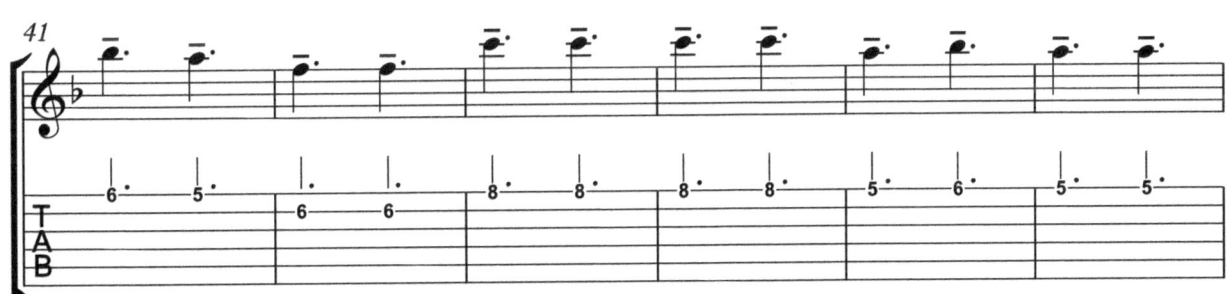

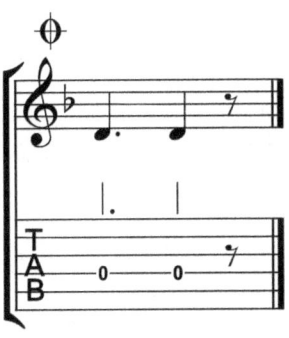

The Miller of Dee

English traditional

Part 1

Molly Malone

Irish traditional

Part 2

Molly Malone

Irish traditional

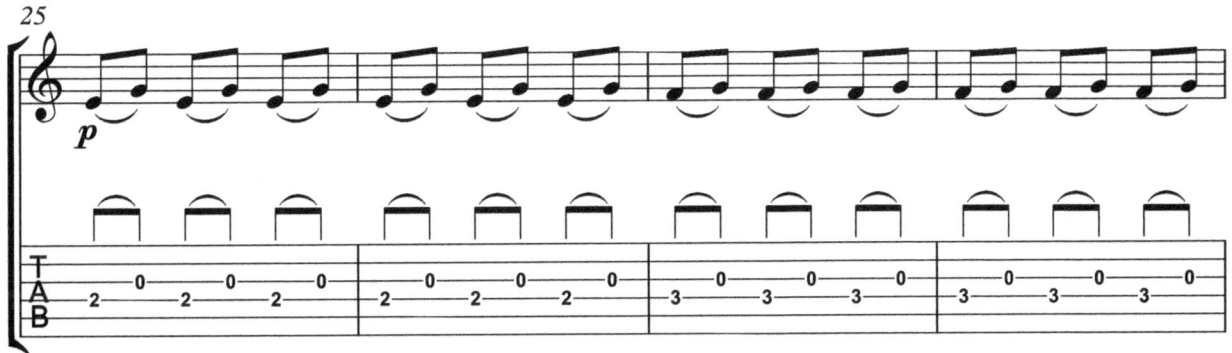
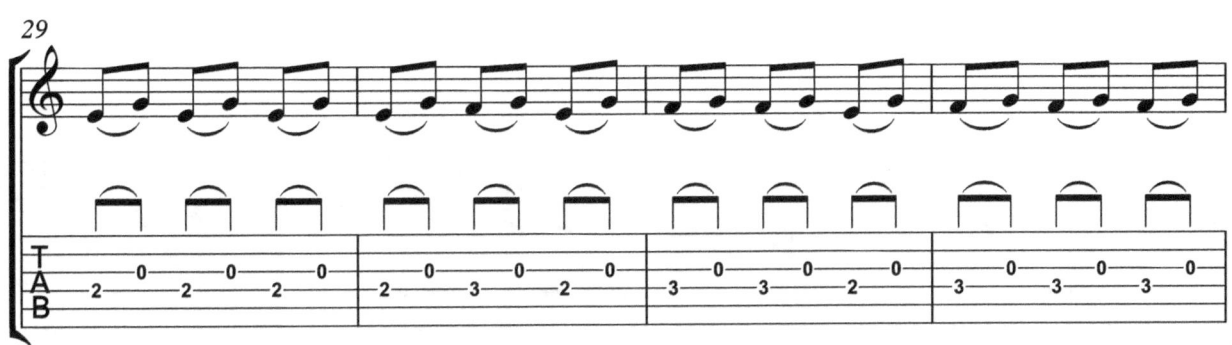
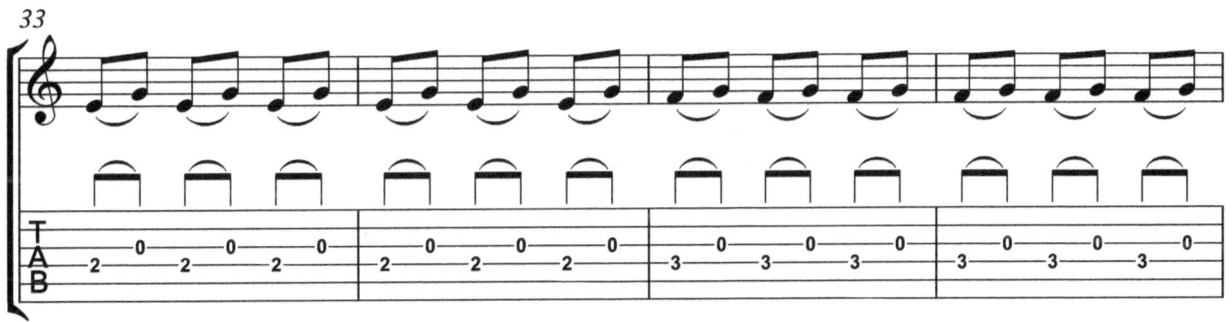
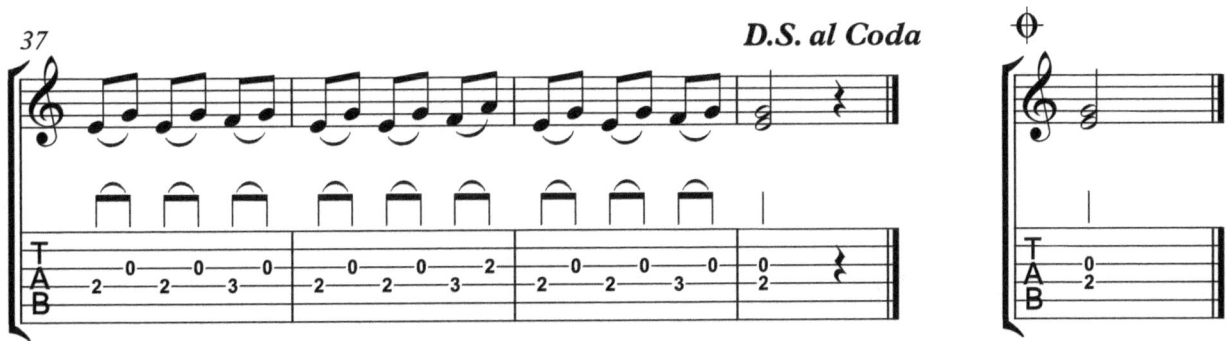

Part 3

Molly Malone

Irish traditional

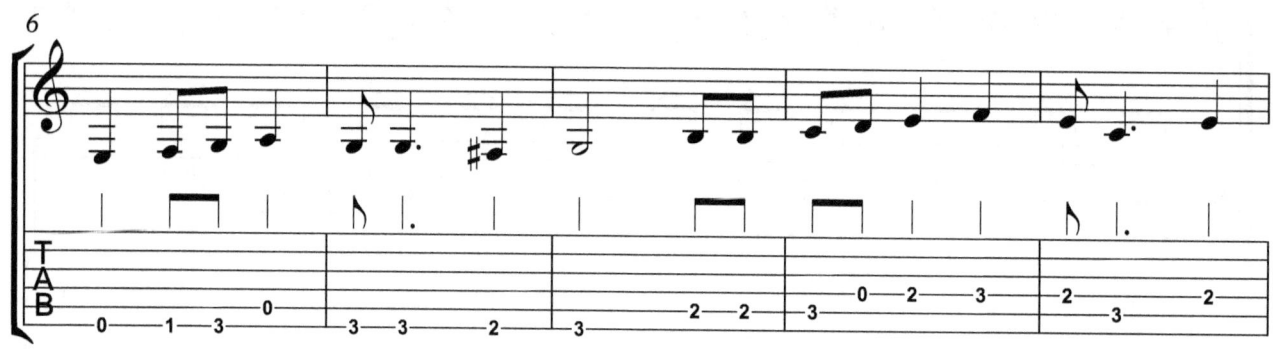

To Coda

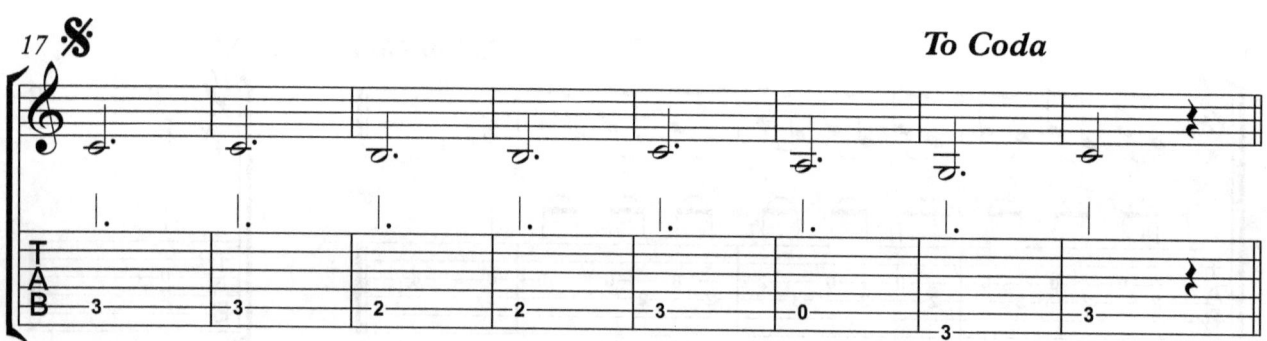

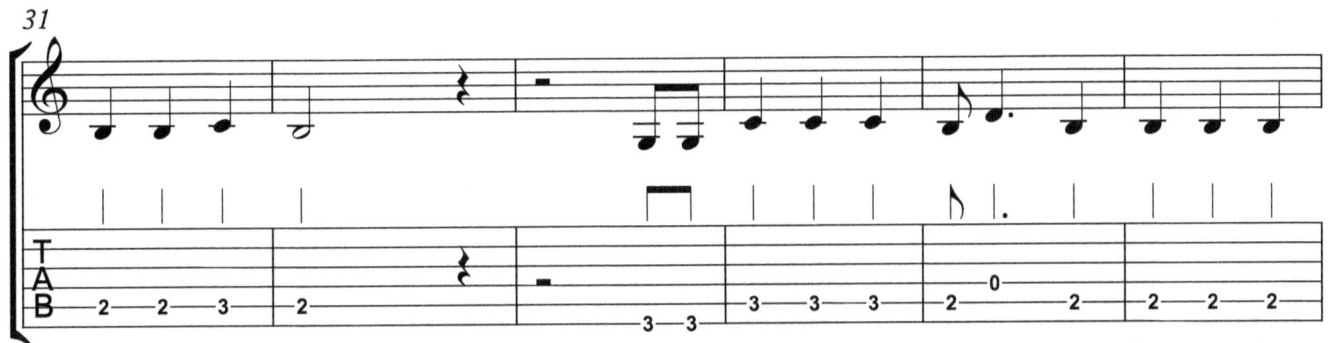

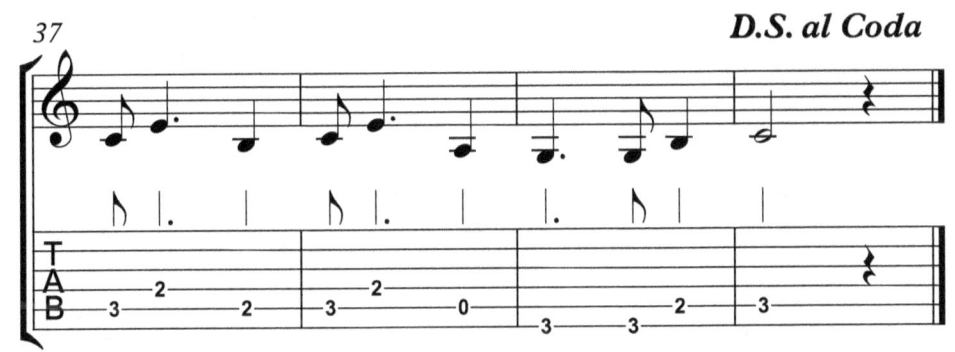

Molly Malone

Irish traditional

Part 1

The Irish Washerwoman

Irish traditional

Part 2

The Irish Washerwoman

Irish traditional

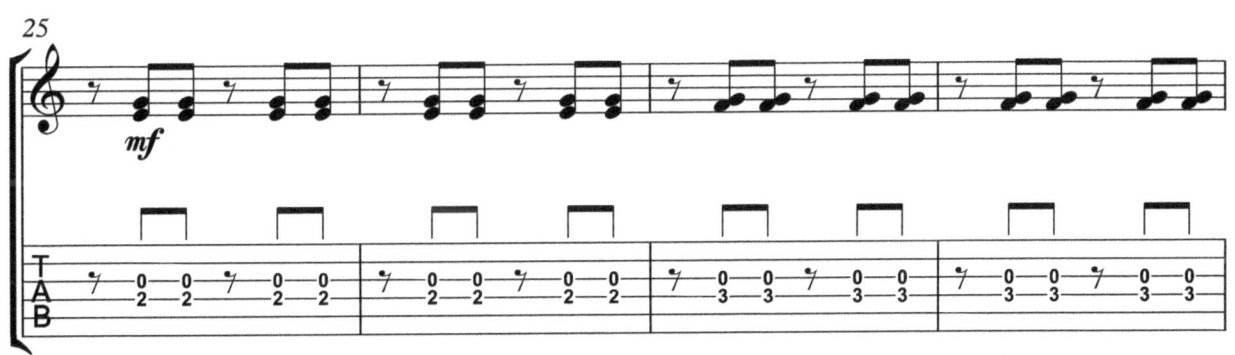

Part 3

The Irish Washerwoman

Irish traditional

Jig

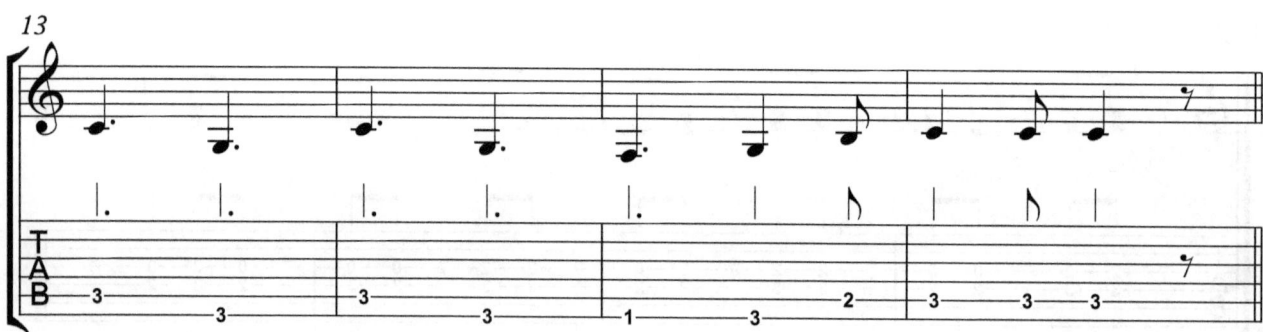

The Irish Washerwoman

Irish traditional

Part 1

The Last Rose of Summer

Irish traditional

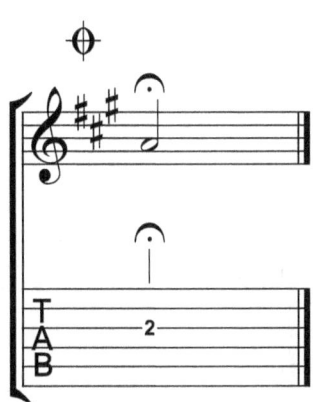

Part 2

The Last Rose of Summer

Irish traditional

Part 3

The Last Rose of Summer

Irish traditional

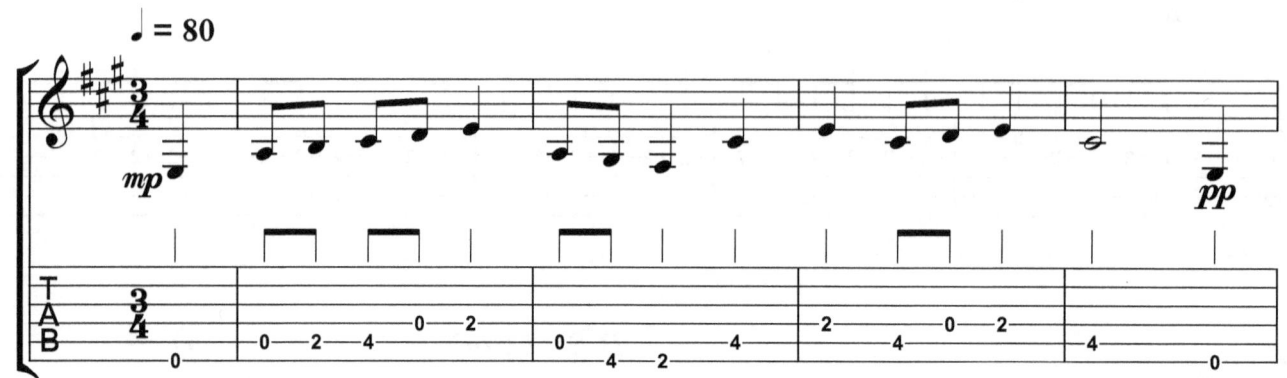

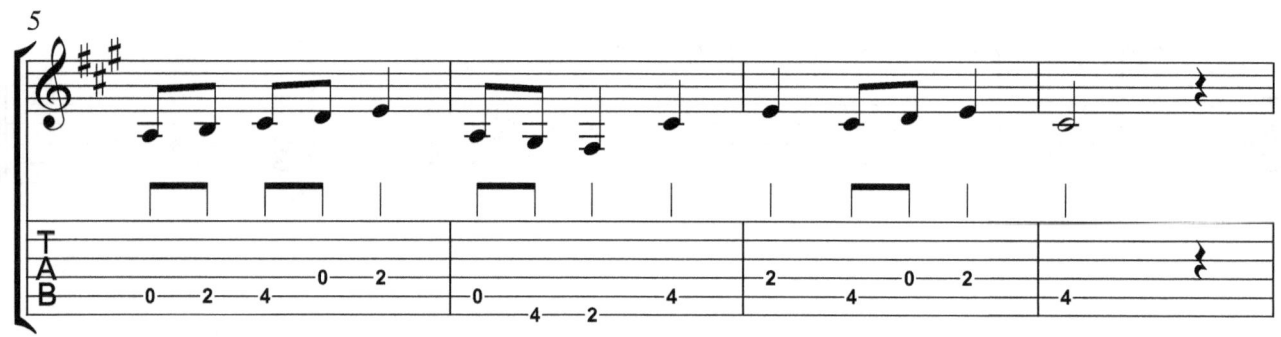

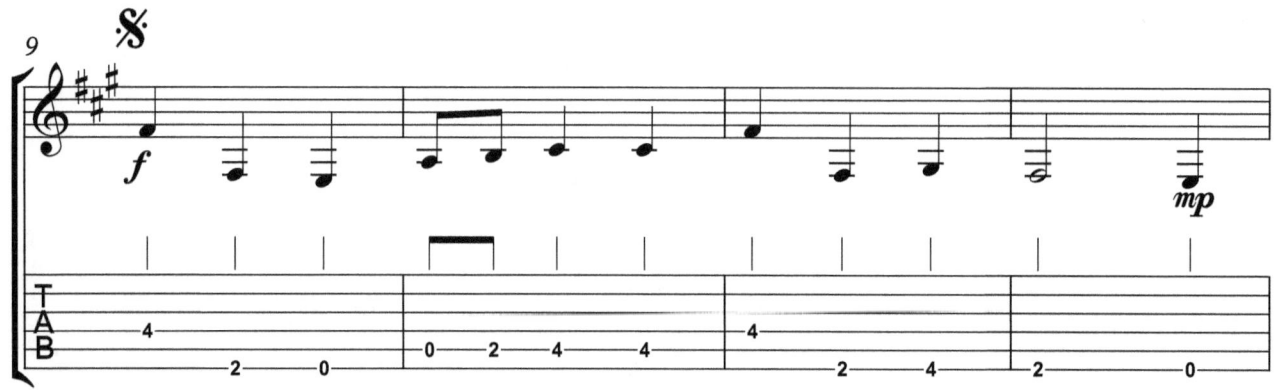

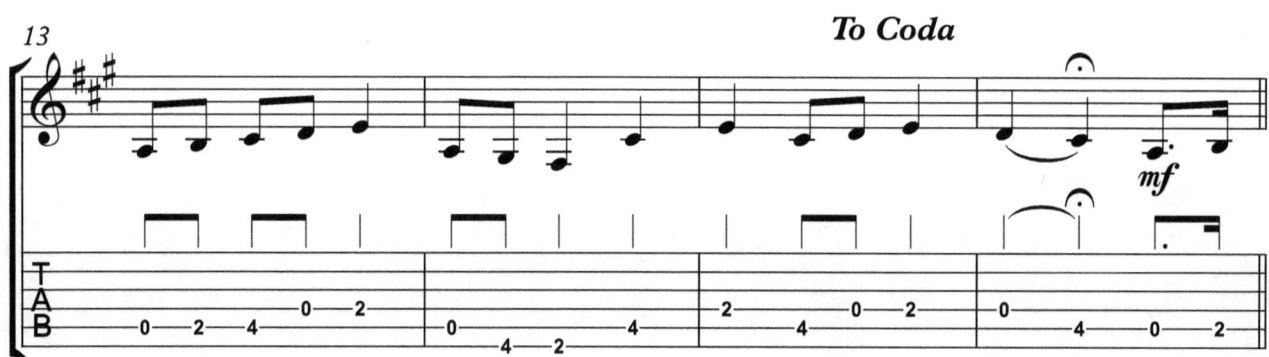

The Last Rose of Summer

Irish traditional

Part 1

Iona Boat Song

Scottish traditional

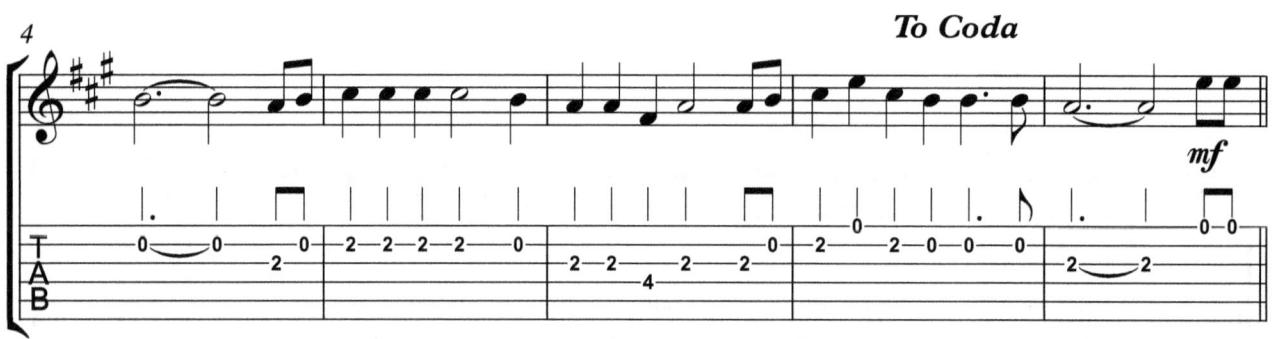

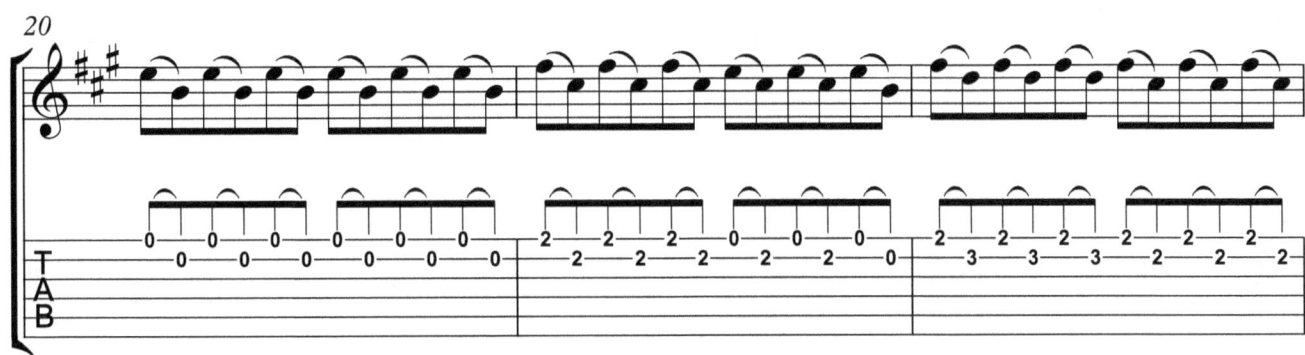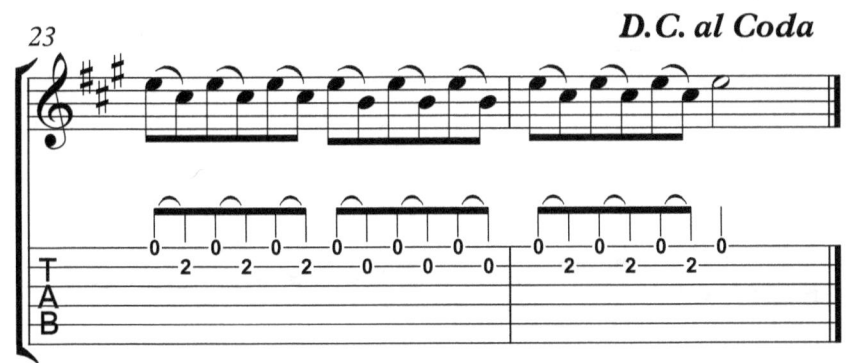

Part 2

Iona Boat Song

Scottish traditional

Iona Boat Song

Part 3

Scottish traditional

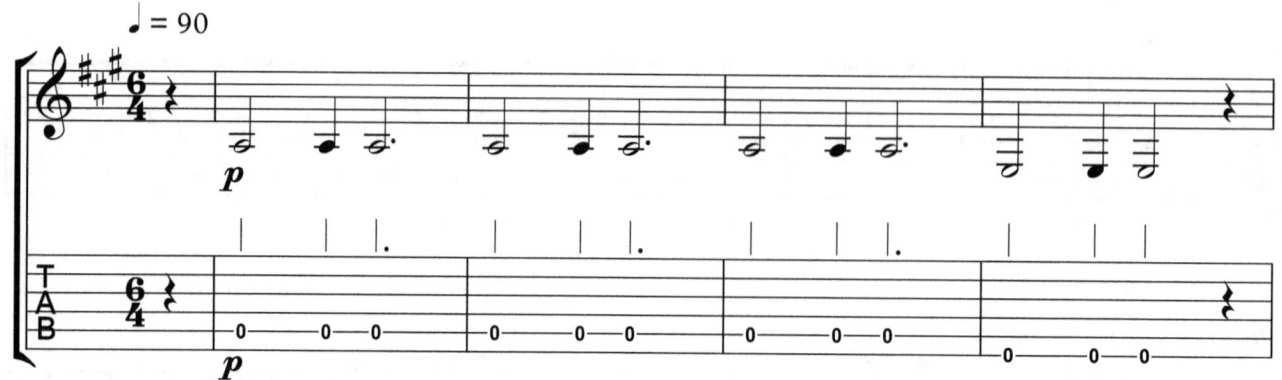

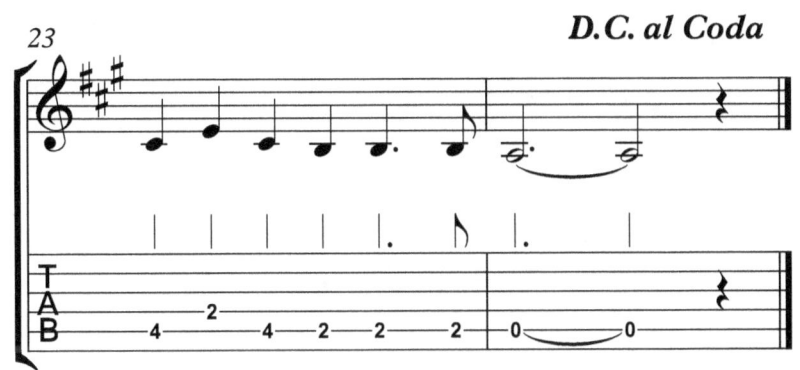

D.C. al Coda

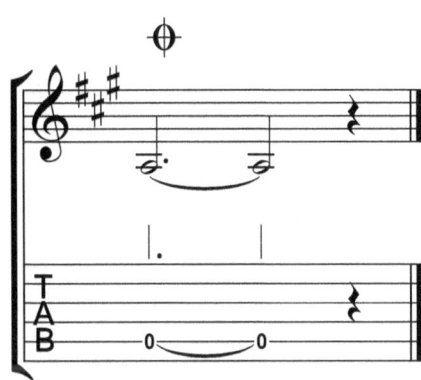

Iona Boat Song

Scottish traditional

Part 1

Loch Lomond

Scottish traditional

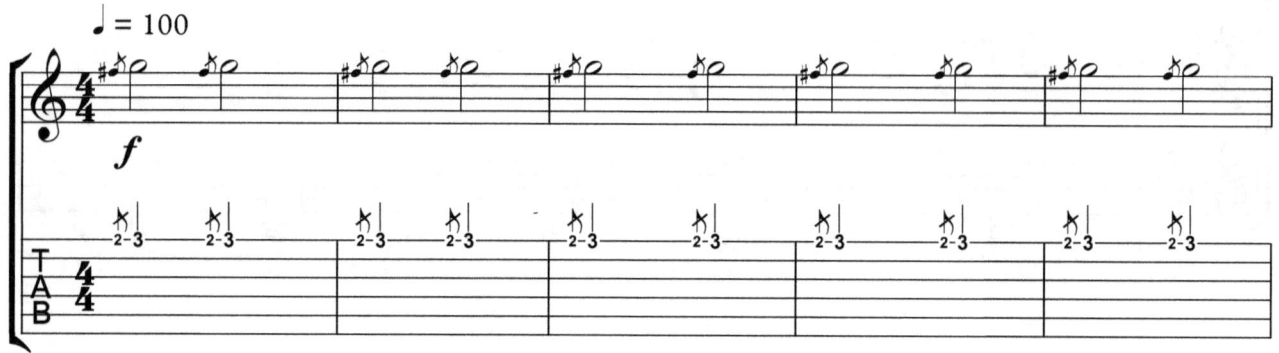
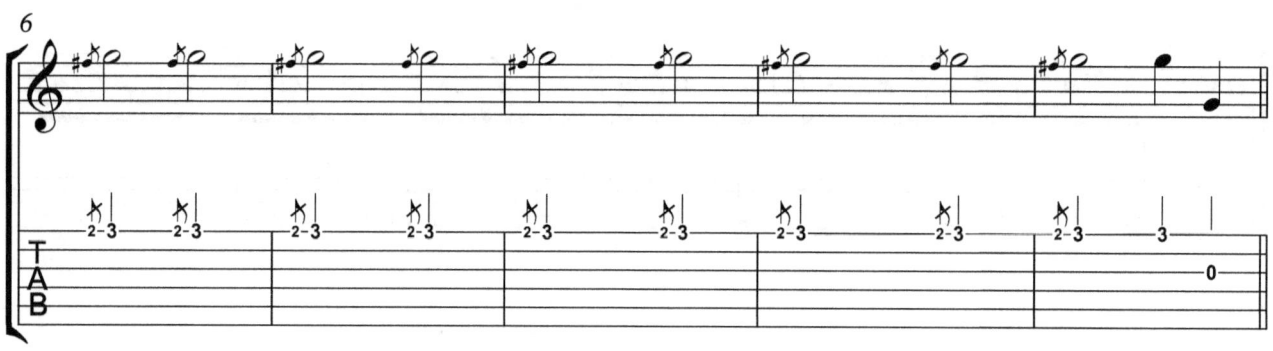

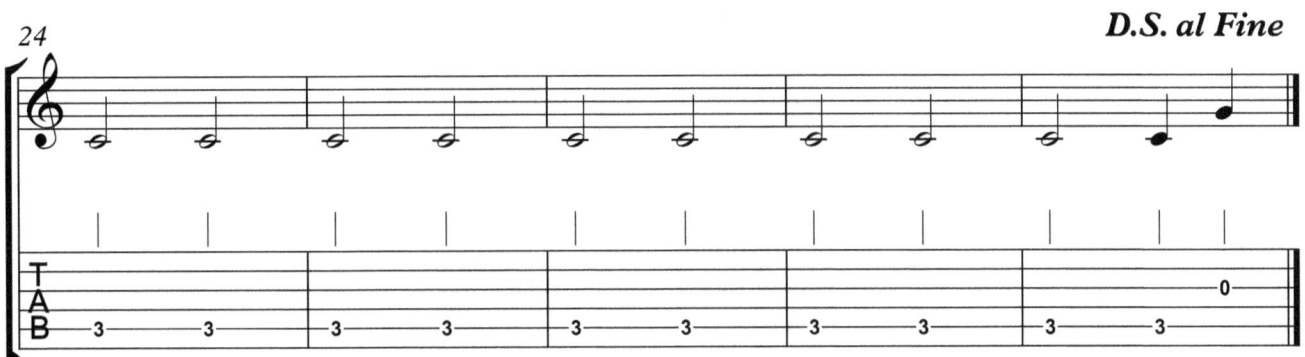

Part 2

Loch Lomond

Scottish traditional

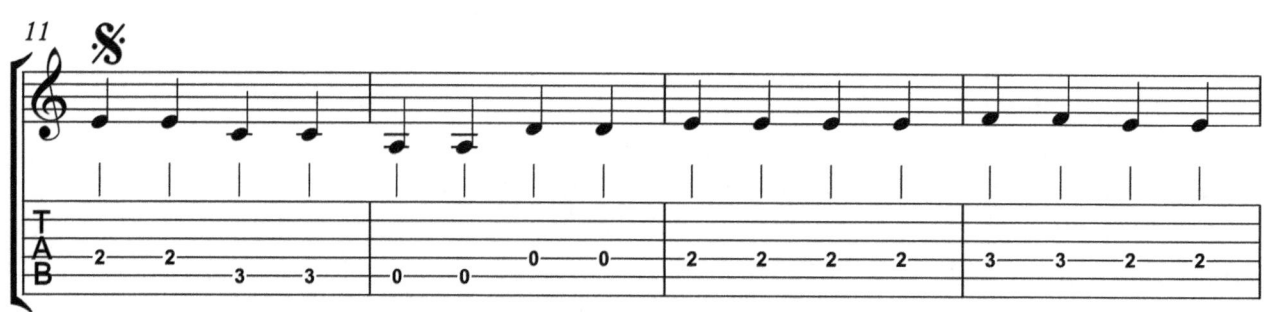
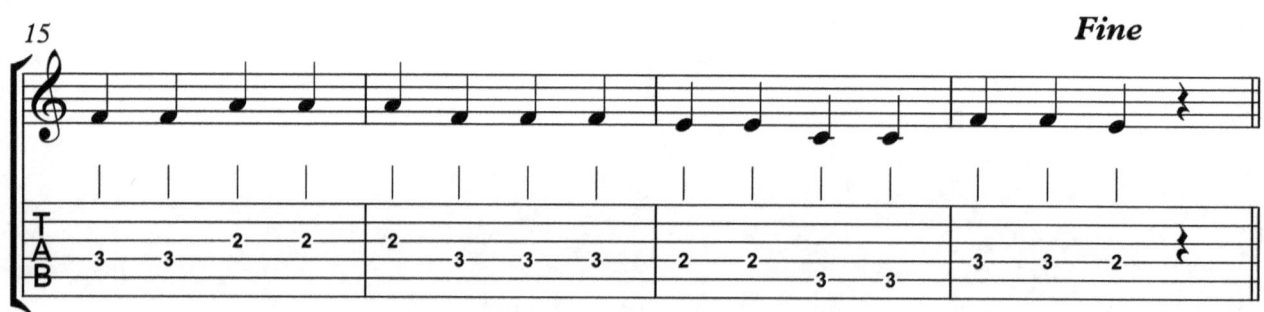

D.S. al Fine

Loch Lomond

Part 3

Scottish traditional

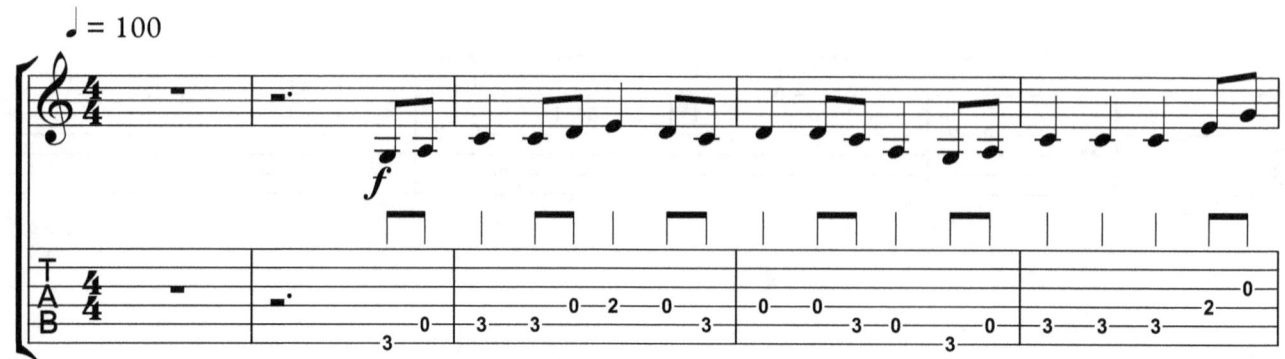
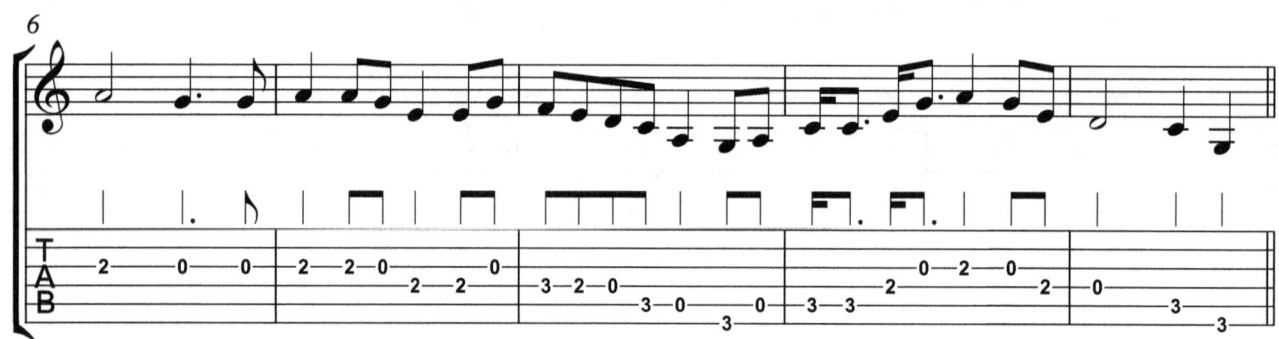
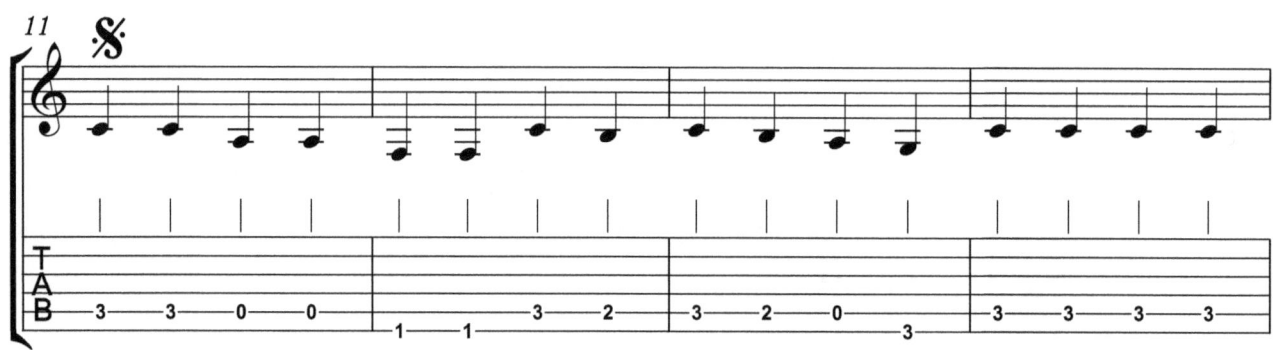
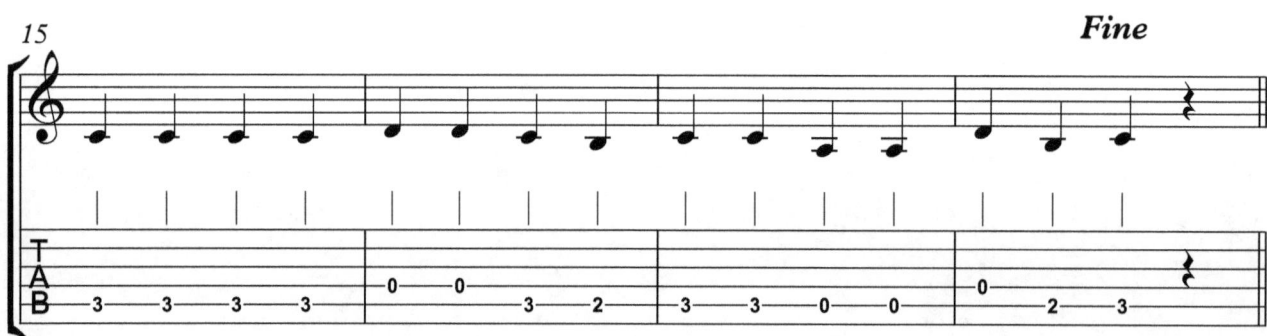

D.S. al Fine

Loch Lomond

Score

Scottish traditional

The Blantyre Explosion

Part 1

Scottish traditional

The Blantyre Explosion

Part 2

Scottish traditional

Part 3

The Blantyre Explosion

Scottish traditional

This page intentionally blank

The Blantyre Explosion

Scottish traditional

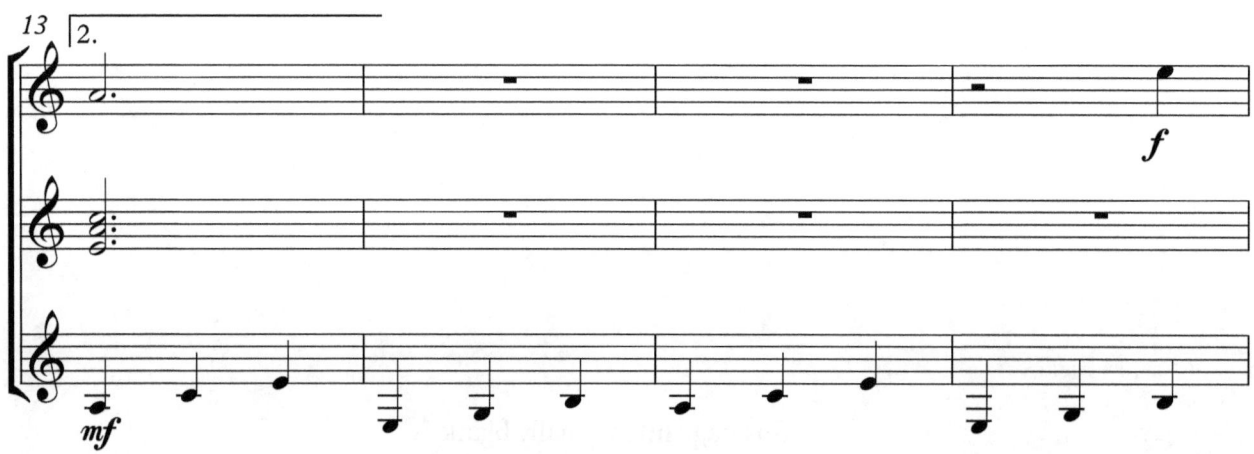

Part 1

All Through the Night

Welsh traditional

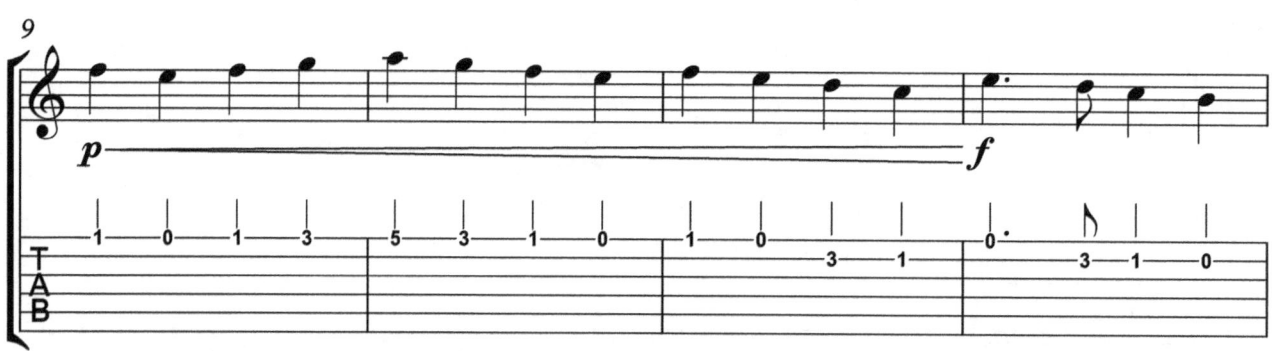

Part 2

All Through the Night

Welsh traditional

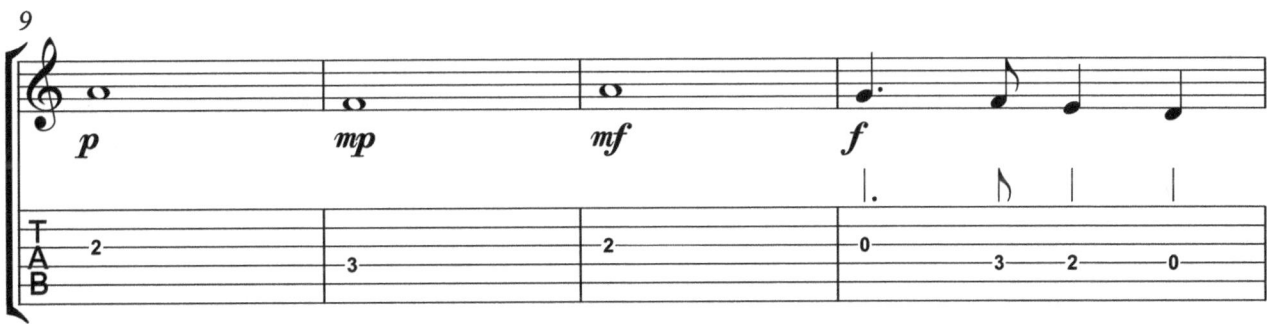

Part 3

All Through the Night

Welsh traditional

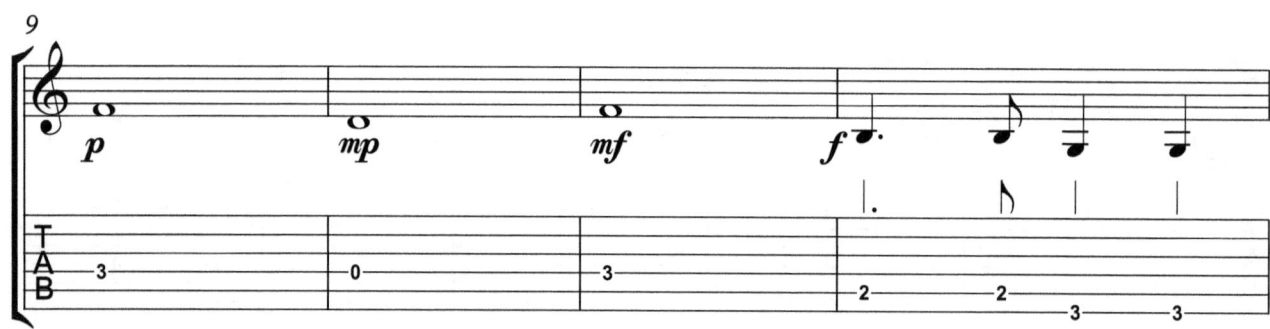

All Through the Night

Welsh traditional

81

Land of my Fathers

Part 1

Wales

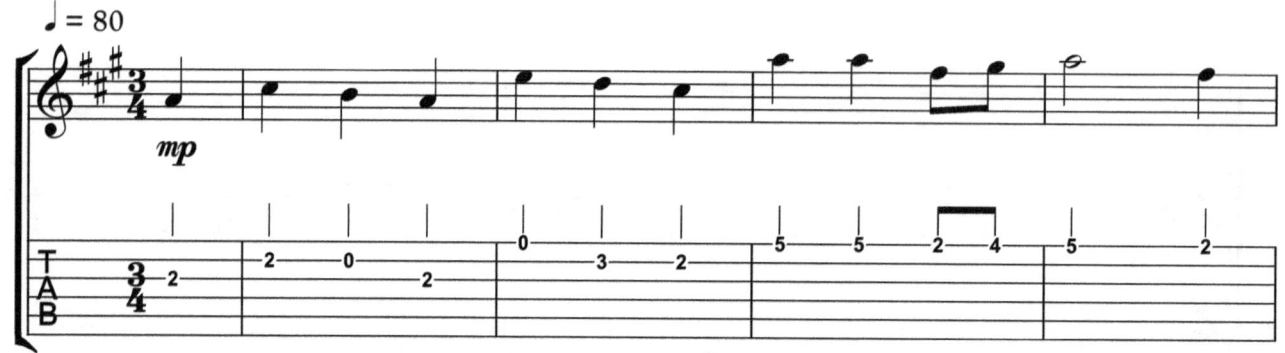

Part 2

Land of my Fathers

Welsh traditional

2

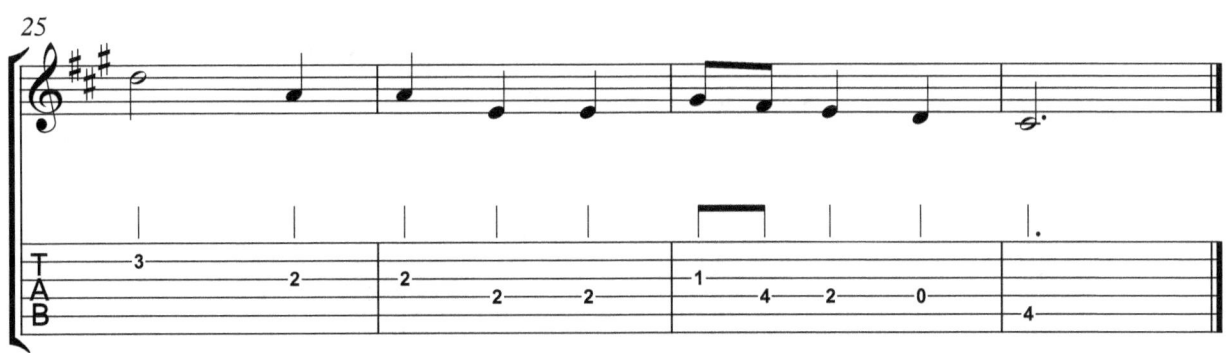

85

Part 3

Land of my Fathers

Welsh traditional

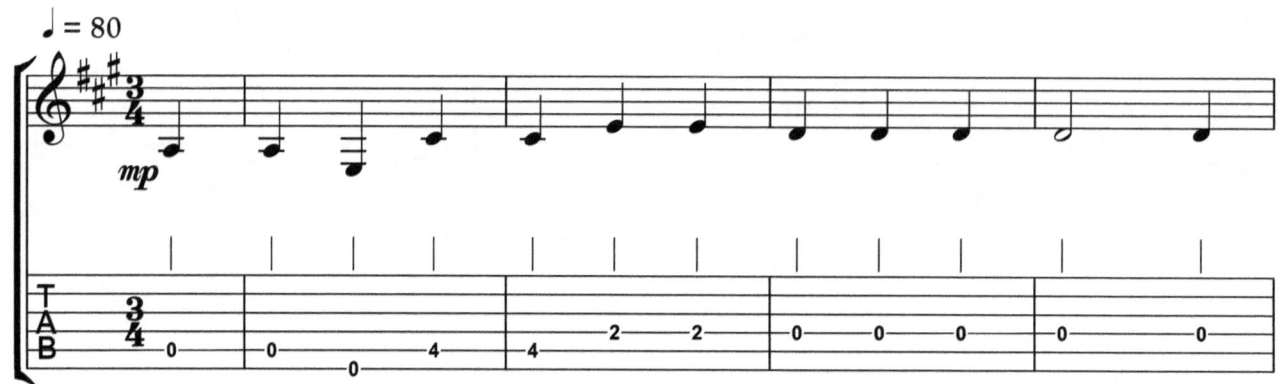
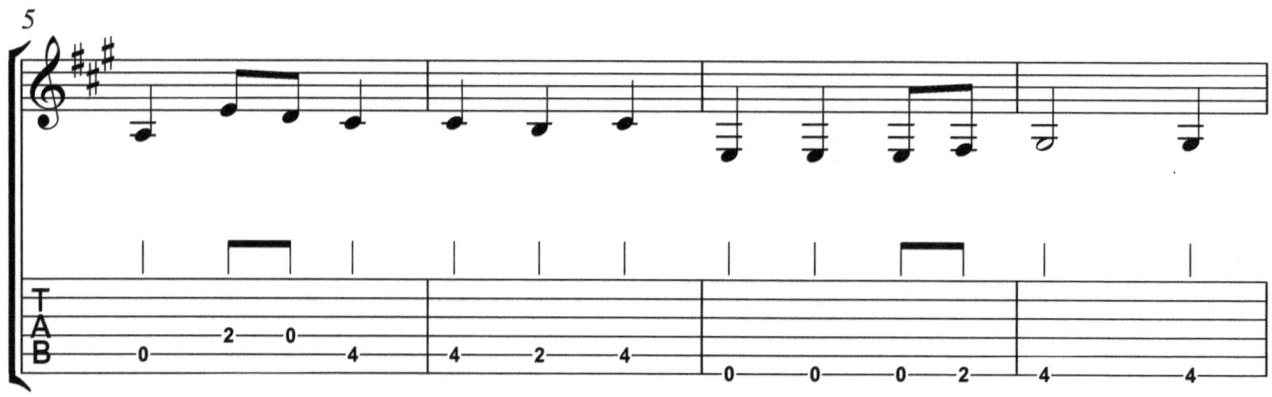
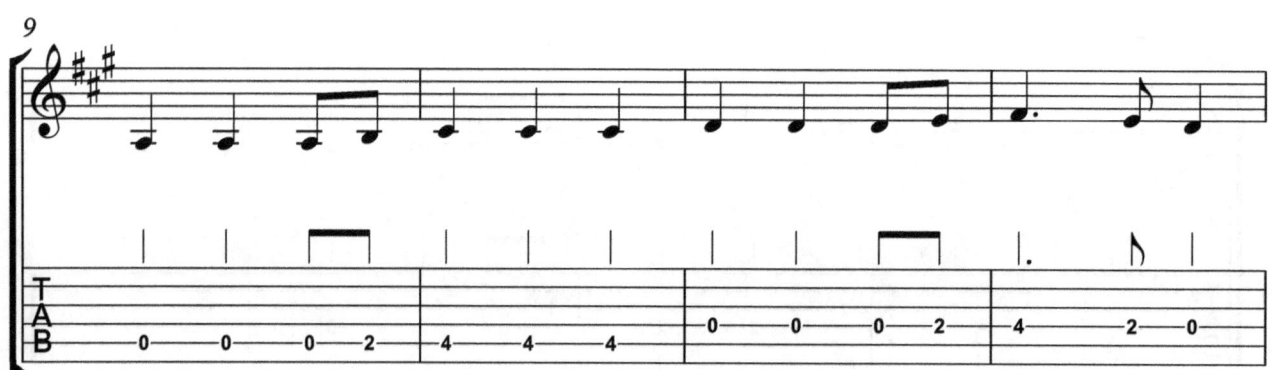

2

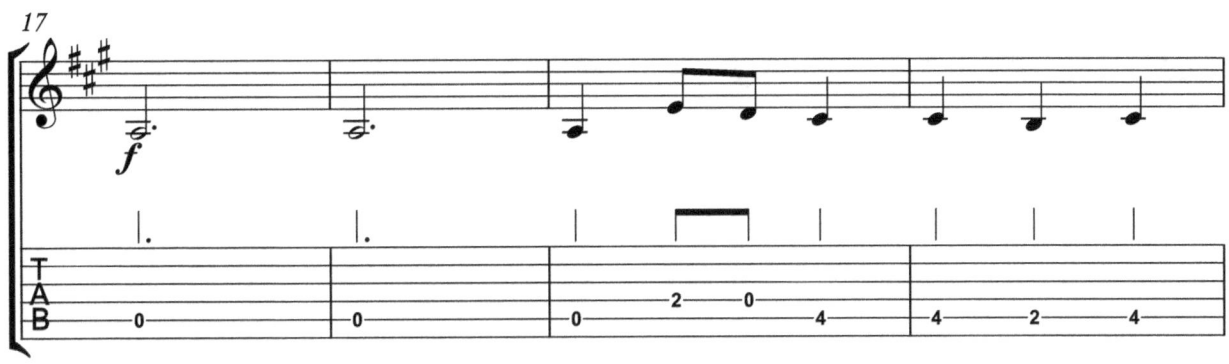

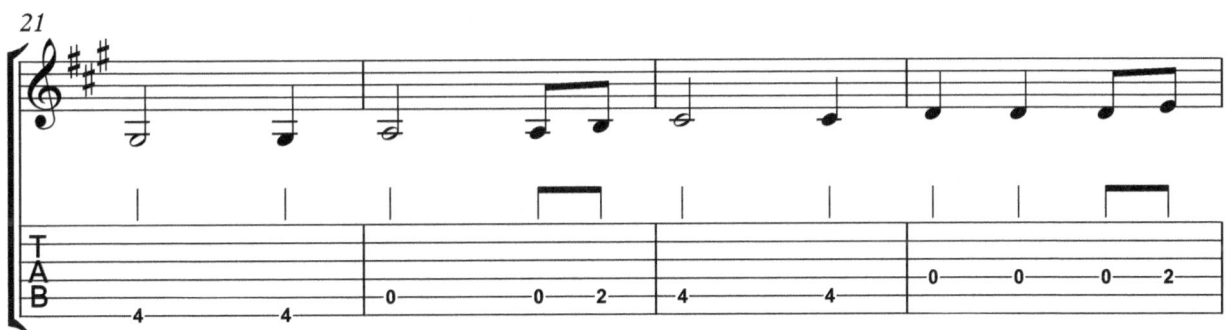

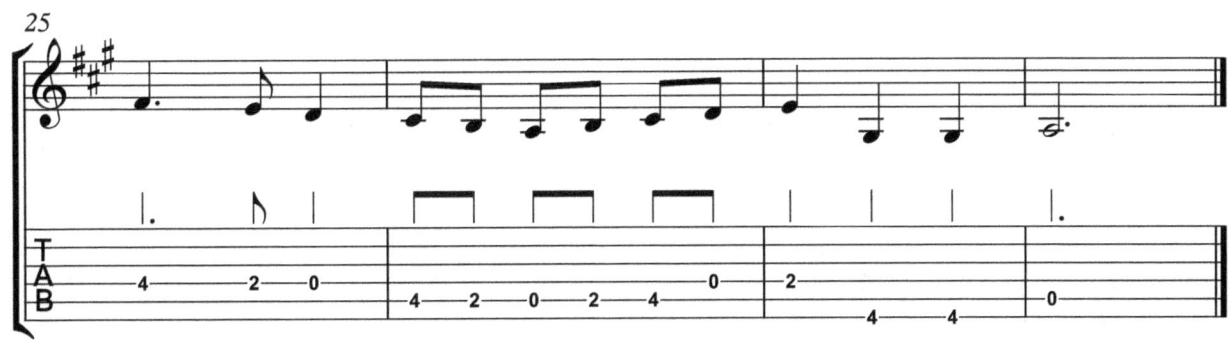

87

Score

Land of my Fathers

Welsh traditional

Part 1

The Ash Grove

Welsh traditional

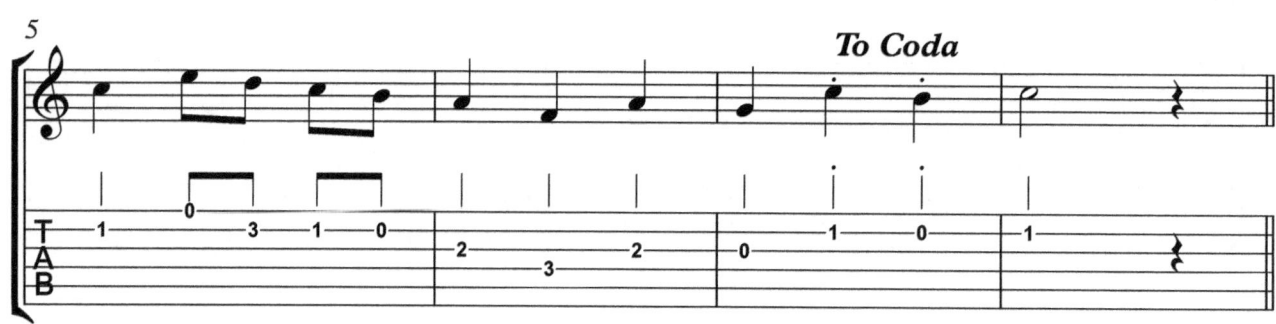

Part 2

The Ash Grove

Welsh traditional

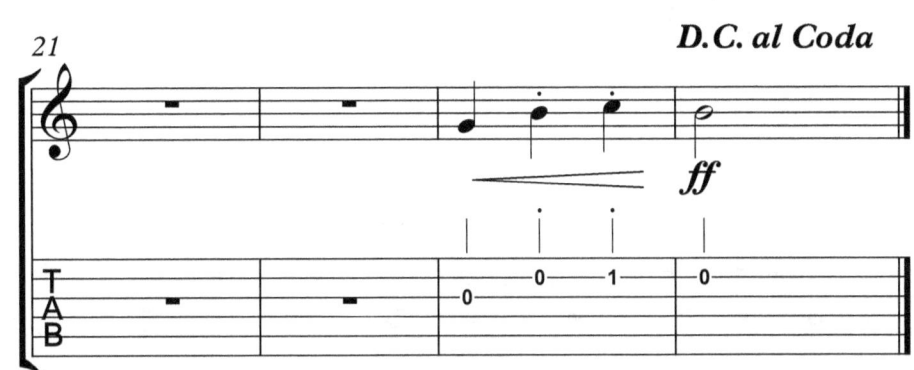
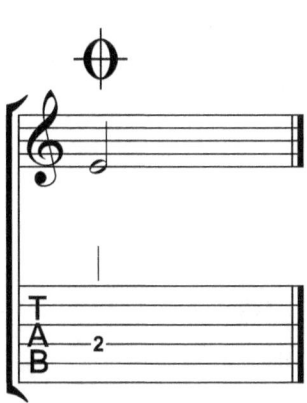

Part 3

The Ash Grove

Welsh traditional

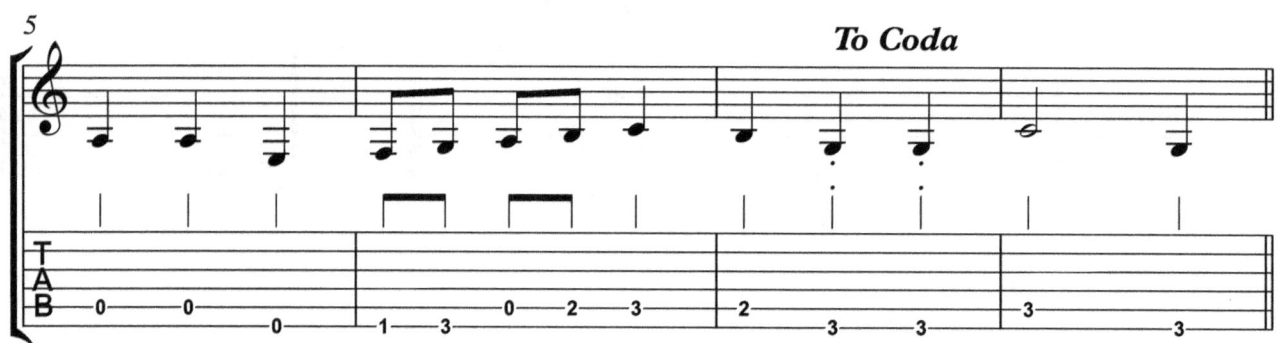

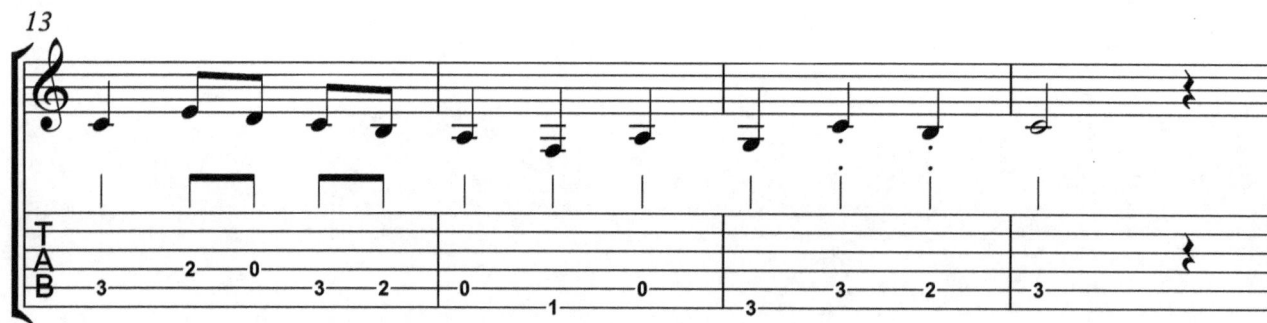

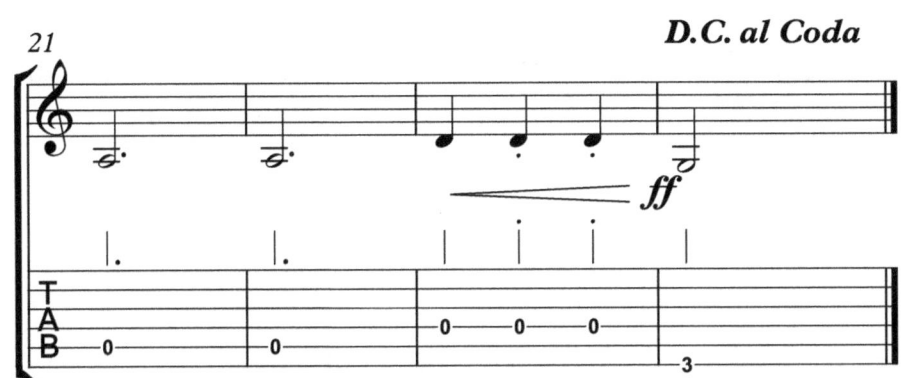
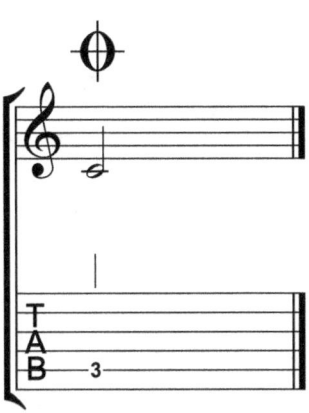

The Ash Grove

Welsh traditional

Other Books from Fundamental Changes

10 Beautiful Classical Pieces Specially Arranged for Guitar Ensemble

Ten Classical Pieces for Guitar Ensemble features 10 well-known, much-loved classical pieces. Together they make up a satisfying performance repertoire for small groups of guitarist to play together. It is often difficult to find works by the great composers written specifically for guitar ensemble, so this book is an essential resource for teachers and students alike.

- 10 pieces of famous classical music, specially transcribed and arranged for small groups of guitarists playing as an ensemble
- Presented in easy-to-read tablature and notation. No need to read music
- Each piece includes a teacher's score and individual parts for 3-4 guitarists

Master 20 Beautiful Classical Guitar Pieces for Beginners

First Pieces for Classical Guitar features 20 carefully selected pieces – each written by a past master of the instrument – aimed at beginners who want to learn to play entire, beautiful pieces. The natural progression of the studies from beginner to intermediate will help you develop your classical guitar language quickly and easily. Notation is included, but each piece is also presented in easy-to-read tablature, so an ability to read music is not necessary.

- 20 beautiful, incremental classical guitar studies
- Playing advice and a breakdown of each classical guitar piece
- Perfectly notated music and guitar tablature with studio-quality audio to download for free.

Master 20 Beautiful Guitar Pieces for Intermediate Players

Intermediate Pieces for Classical Guitar features 20 carefully selected pieces – each written by a past master of the instrument – aimed at Intermediate players who want to learn to play entire, pieces. The natural progression of the studies from Intermediate to intermediate will help you develop your classical guitar language quickly and easily. Notation is included, but each piece is also presented in easy-to-read tablature, so an ability to read music is not necessary.

- Learn 20 great classical guitar pieces written by legends of the instrument
- Presented in easy-to-read tablature and notation. No need to read music
- Includes helpful analysis and breakdown of each piece, along with its historical background